The Youth Leadership Empowerment System

The
Youth
Leadership
Empowerment
System™

Volume 1
First edition

Bryan Berkeley, CPL

# Copyrights & License

Publisher:

CM BERKELEY MEDIA GROUP

Ontario, Canada

First Edition

The Youth Leadership Empowerment System.
Print ISBN: 978-0-9811493-2-5
Digital ISBN: 978-0-9868018-7-7

Copyright

Copyright(c)2013 Bryan Berkeley. All rights reserved. Without limiting the rights under copyright reserved above, no part of this publication may be reproduced, stored in or introduced into a retrieval system, or transmitted, in any form, or by any means (electronic, mechanical, photocopying, recording, or otherwise) without the prior written permission of both the copyright owner and the above publisher of this book.

Any resemblance to characters, places, brands, media, and incidents are purely coincidental. The author acknowledges the trademarked status and trademark owners of various products referenced in this work, which have been used without permission. The publication/use of these trademarks is not authorized, associated with, or sponsored by the trademark owners.

Digital Edition License Notes

The book is licensed for your individual personal enjoyment only. The ebook version may not be re-sold or given away to other people. If you would like to share this book with another person, please purchase an additional copy for each person you share it with. If you're reading this book and did not purchase it, or it was not purchased for your use only, then you should return to Amazon.com and purchase your own copy. Thank you for respecting the author's work.

Bryan Berkeley

The Youth Leadership Empowerment System (YLES)

This online training program consists of the following components:

- Bi-weekly motivational email
- Personal Amazing Stories from Bryan
- Youth Peer Members
- Access to Exclusive Membership Area
- YLES Online Training
- Video Resources
- Audio Resources
- Tools to Help You Get Your Life Together
- And More as We Grow

The Youth Leadership Empowerment System

All parents and youth need to get access to this program as a foundation for a better and brighter future.

* * * * *

Reviews from Readers Like You

"Bryan's book is a great read for teens and young adults alike. Well done Bryan!"
- Jenny Berkeley, Best-Selling Author, Magazine Publisher

"It's hard to believe, in reading this book, that the writer is not much older with all of the wisdom and maturity he relates. At the same time his stories are entertaining and relatable for all ages. He seems to have unlocked secrets that so many of us can use in life – especially those who are questioning what leadership is and what it takes to become a great leader!" ~ Jean Booth

"Bryan shows that leadership is not about being in charge; it is about setting a goal and reaching it with perseverance. He encourages everyone to make the most out of every situation for the common good. Dedication to excellence is what Bryan is all about." ~ Dan Capozzi

"Bryan, I'm really proud of your accomplishments as a young man. You're already a success because you have helped many people in life and are doing what you love. This book is awesome. I know you'll reach more young people." ~ Vaughn Berkeley

* * * * *

The Youth Leadership Empowerment System

More Great Books from CMBMG

CM Berkeley Media Group, based in Canada, works with its authors to produce books which help to uplift the human spirit, spread the message of health and wellness, and offer practical insights in finances, and other areas. We also offer services to help authors convert their books to Kindle or ePUB format, get their book edited, and get a great cover design, and other services for indie authors.

Facebook Fan Page: cmberkeleymediagroup
Website: www.cmberkeleymediagroup.com
Email: info@cmberkeleymediagroup.com

Check out other great titles from our authors:

<u>Eating4Eternity: Unlock Your Holistic Health Lifestyle™</u>

<u>Sweet Raw Desserts: Life Is Sweet Raw™</u>

Can I Offer You A Cigarette: The Only Sure Way To Break The Smoking Habit

Fresh Food4Life™: The Case For Taking Back Control of Your Food And Empowering Your Family And Community.

The Adventures of Moshe Monkey and Elias Froggy: A Healthy Business

Colon By Design: Overcoming The Stigma Of Colon Sickness And Unlocking True Colon Health™ ISBN-

Bryan Berkeley

13: 978-0-9868018-1-5 (Coming Soon)

* * * * *

Want to become a published author in 90 days? CM Berkeley Media Group has an online training program to help anyone aspiring to achieve this dream. Find out more about it and realize your dream at
http://cmberkeleymediagroup.com/writeyourbookin90days/

Dedication

This book is dedicated to
my mom who has always been
a supporter of my dreams.

Thank you mom for everything
you did and continue to do.

* * * * *

Acknowledgement

Over the years, I've met many people who have had a positive influence in my life. While many people have their faults, there are times in their lives when they too can shine, if given a chance. And so, I want to use this opportunity to mention a few people I've met who have shined in my presence. I wish them all many more moments to shine. For those unmentioned, I want you to know, you're not forgotten.

Mary Berkeley	Vaughn Berkeley
Jenny Berkeley	Zac Joseph
Mr. D. Capozzi	Mr. Geradi
Ms. Mezitti	Mr. Chin You
Nicole Bennoit	Mrs. S. DePallo
Ms. S. Marino	Mr. DeAngelo
Mr. Kreves	Ms. Douglas
Mr. Hamylin	Mr. Fox

I'd also like to thank Brebouf High School Teachers and Principal, and the members of the Toronto Catholic District School Board for the connections made.

Last but not least, I'd like to thank my commanding officers in the Canadian Armed Forces. Military life is great and the men and women who serve our God and country in the ranks deserve our respect and admiration.

Nitendo Vinces

The Youth Leadership Empowerment System

Table of Contents

Dedication ix

Acknowledgement x

Foreword 2

Introduction 6

Paying For Peace 8

No One Left Behind 14

Monte Casino - All Jobs 19

The Bus Story 24

The Bus Fare Story 32

Changes on the Fly (BWW Kidnapping) 37

Leadership Knows No Boundaries 43

Making Yourself Job Ready 50

Diet and Health 58

Money Smarts For Youth 68

A Youth Action Plan 87

Conclusion 94

* * * *

Foreword

A 15-year-old girl lies in the foetal position on her bed with her hands pressed against her ears, wishing she couldn't hear her screaming parents through the walls. Her plush duvet isn't comforting enough to withstand the ache in her heart.

A soldier presses two, plastic ear buds – which used to be white, but are now covered in dull, latte-colored dust – hard into his skull, praying for just a little more juice from his iPod battery so it can drown out some of the cacophony Indirect Fire making its own music overhead.

A teenaged couple silently cries together as they desperately try to comfort their screaming baby, each thinking they wish they had a dependable parent to turn to at that very moment. They make no eye contact, and stare through one another as their minds wander toward a quieter, make-believe world.

What do these three seemingly entirely different people have in common? Conflict. Challenge. Choice.

In this excellent work written by Bryan Berkeley, through true stories of his own, he encourages youth like him to be leaders, be inspired, and make authentic choices. His stories are relevant, poignant, and universal.

I can relate to Bryan on so many levels. Although I am older than him, a female, and a US citizen, I, too, was in the military and I, too, have stopped and started purpose-driven professional projects many times. This work is a culmination of his persistence and a gift to the world. I admire his determination and how he is able to illustrate the practical application of core character traits throughout his book because knowledge is not power in and of itself unless you are equipped to act upon that knowledge. Bryan inspires action.

As Bryan says, "We have to roll with the flow, adapt, and pursue the thing we desire if that is truly where our joy lies." This reminds me so much of one of the United States Marine Corps mantras, "Adapt and overcome," but I love how Bryan used the qualities he learned both growing up and whilst in the military to apply to his current success and leadership in a way that is not a pithy regurgitation of military rhetoric.

I appreciate that Bryan has the wherewithal to incorporate the values of love, forgiveness, peace, purpose and movement forward into all of his stories and pieces of wisdom imparted.

I truly admire Bryan for what he's doing. He is being a leader by action, not just by word or claim.

"Bad things happen sometimes. However, the past is the past and nothing we can do will change it. So move forward in a positive way with a lesson learned," Bryan says. This is the message of my book "Just Roll With It: The 7 Battle-Tested Traits for Creating a Ridiculously Happy, Healthy, and Successful Life."

So, naturally, I agree whole-heartedly with one of the main

themes of his book, which is to move forward in a spirit of learning and love no matter what hand you've been dealt.

Ultimately, you have the power of choice to live the life you love and love the life you live. This message certainly resonates in the mind, body, and spirit of us all, doesn't it?

The Youth Leadership Empowerment System is a book that is thoroughly enjoyable and exactly what today's youth need to give them a head start on a path to developing their leader within. Bryan Berkeley has the makings of a master storyteller but most amazingly is that the stories are his stories.

For a young man he has lived some great moments and lets us into his world for a brief but awesome moment. I know that I would have appreciated this book as a young person myself and am positive that many teens, young adults, and adults in their twenties will enjoy this book.

Here's to being inspired and empowered from this moment forward! Just Roll With It™! ;)

Sarah Plummer

Author, Just Roll With It: The 7 Battle-Tested Traits for Creating a Ridiculously Happy, Healthy, and Successful Life

Founder,www.SemperSarah.com

Creator,www.JustRollWithItBootcamp.com which

The Youth Leadership Empowerment System

benefits military, veterans, and their families, friends, and communities. In partnership with the non-profit group, www.TeamRWB.org, scholarships are available for this seminar series and corresponding week-long retreats.

* * * * *

Introduction

Why did I put together this book? The short answer is that I wanted to help more people and reach more people. The long answer is that I believe that we all have a purpose and a calling in life. I have always been the kind of guy to help my friends and family out.

In short, I care. I care about how my peers are doing at home, at school and in the community. And I wrote this book because I care about you. I want more young people to be leaders even if they came from a poor family, or had a hard life, or were abused, or become a teenage parent, or suffered some other difficult life event.

I truly believe that leadership principles can impact every area of your life for the better. And with this belief, I had a plan to write this book. I actually had the idea for it in 2008 and started it in that year.

Then I stopped, then started, then stopped, then started. And it went like this for a while because my military life, along with other priorities in life kept pushing the book back. I was almost ready to launch it by the end of 2012 but hit another snag that led to a delay.

But all this just shows that such is life. As leaders, we have to roll with the flow, adapt, and pursue the thing we desire if that is truly where our joy lies.

And so this book is written and published. I believe that

everything happens in the right time and so now is the time for the book to be on the scene and now is the time for you to have it.

I wish you the best as you read my book and I look forward to meeting you as the leader you were meant to be.

Love,
Bryan Berkeley

* * * * *

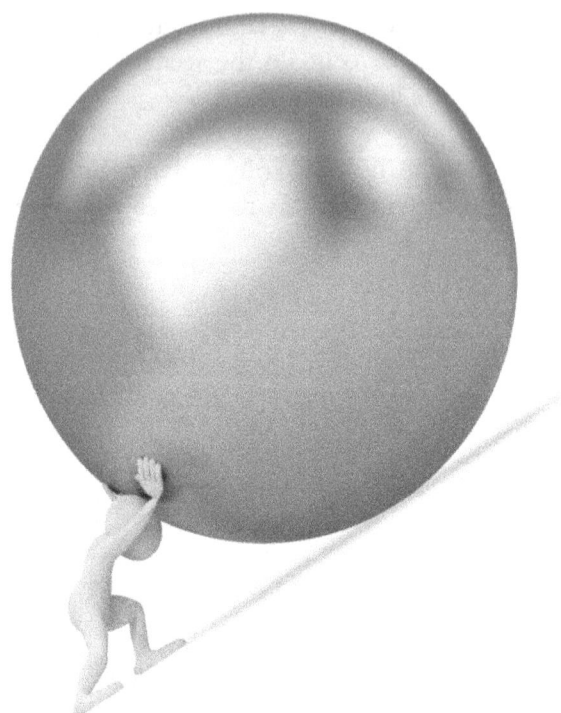

Paying For Peace

Early in my second year of high school one of my school friends was playing a joke on another kid in school and took his PSP. The joker put the PSP in my locker. I thought it was his PSP. Much later the boy who was the owner of the PSP told the principal that his PSP was stolen. The investigation began.

On the school security camera it looked like my school friend had taken the PSP and put it in my locker. Had I known about this prank, I would not have allowed it as I am opposed to these kinds of foolish actions.

On the camera another school kid who vaguely looked like me went into the locker and took the PSP and left school. To the principal, it looked like me. I told the principal who it was but the guilty person denied it. When I asked, that is, insisted that I wanted to look at the school video surveillance, it mysteriously vanished yet we were still accused. For the sake of peace, I ended up paying to replace a PSP that I was framed and wrongfully accused of taking.

This was the beginning of the turning point in my life. I decided that I would stand up for justice in the future wherever I was able because no one stood up for me.

~ ~ ~ ~ ~ ~ ~ ~

"I would rather die standing than live on my knees!" – Emiliano Zapata

"Don't back down just to keep the peace. Standing up for your beliefs builds self-confidence and self-esteem." – Oprah Winfrey

"I know that our choices influence our outcomes. Leaders need to make the right choices without fear of failing but if it fails, learn from it and move on." – Bryan Berkeley

~ ~ ~ ~ ~ ~ ~ ~

Leaders learn from their mistakes.

I thought I would start the book off with this story

because it shows a turning point. It shows that at times when a situation seems at its worst, it can be the beginning of a better path in life.

For me, I was foolish to have allowed my locker to be part of any prank but I didn't know what was taking place to begin with. So my ignorance came with a heavy price. I had to fork out money for a PSP that I never came into contact with. Sometimes I still think of that situation and think what manner of madness is that!

However, I have put it behind me. My life is much better now because I resolved to stand up for justice. I paid the price for peace and it cost more than dollars. But we live in a fair world where God works it all out in the grand scheme of things. I'm sure my Catholic School religion teachers would agree to this.

I experienced things working out because I am now a leader among my peers. I am respected by parents, teachers, my fellow students, my own family and most importantly, ME. Get this straight, I'm not blowing my own horn. I simply love who I have grown up to become and I love what being among positive influences has done in my life. I also love being in the military which is the coolest place to be. I am surrounded by leaders, that is, the commanding officers. I am surrounded by potential leaders, that is, my peers and myself included. And we all have the opportunity to be the best we can be while being paid. How great is that!

Now before parents think my book is a recruiting tool for the Canadian Armed Forces, I assure you that it was not intended to be. However, I certainly won't object to the army purchasing copies and using it in their recruiting programs. My book is written from my own experience and how these experiences show leadership for me.

My stories of leadership could very well be the story for your own son or daughter. As a parent, you may simply have missed it because in your mind, you still see your little baby instead of a budding leader. That's okay. Most parents will eventually grow out of it.

As for young people, my book is written for you because I want to help any young person who will read this book. My own life has changed because of the positive influences of my family, my school teachers, the military and my own willingness to be better. Your life can change too. Don't let anyone put you down. Not even the reflection in the mirror.

If you make a mistake, which is something we all do, just pick yourself up, dust yourself off and move forward.

Sometimes the cost of a mistake is very high and this cost is one you have to live with if you made such a mistake. This could be two youths having to live with a new baby due to teenage pregnancy or a young person with a disability caused by driving recklessly on the roads or any other tragic event.

One member of my training unit died the Canadian Victoria Day weekend of 2008. His car crashed.

This was a sad day for all of us in the unit. In May of 2009 I visited his grave site with my buddy. His parents came to the site the same day. They looked at me and said that I looked familiar. I said that I was in the same unit as their son and they would have seen me at the funeral.

The mother was more intent. She said that there was something more. Then it hit her. She pulled out the last and most loved picture they have of their lost son. She showed me the picture and I was in the picture with their son. Every time the family looked at that picture to remember him, they also saw me. I got goose pimples because I was a part of something so precious to them. They were also glad to see that I remembered their son, my friend, by visiting his grave.

Bad things happen sometimes. However, the past is past and nothing we can do will change it. So move forward in a positive way with a lesson learned. If you are a teenage parent and have a baby, then you have to grow up fast and take care of it the best you can. If you were injured in an accident, you need to structure your life to overcome your disabilities.

If you made a mistake, and you are genuine in your heart, then don't let society punish you forever for it. Forgive yourself. For example, the church may make a teenage parent feel terrible for sinning and people may shun the youth. Well, my advice is to take your licks for now. Learn from the experience.

And move past it because the earth still turns and life still goes on.

If you were lucky and no dramatic, life-changing event took place but you still want to be better, then go for it. This just proves that your dramatic, life-changing event took place in your mind and spirit.

My brother, who is many years older than me, went to high school where the motto was "Nitendo Vinces". I thought it would be nice to use it because this means, "By striving, we will conquer." My brother was an average kid like me but he has always persisted in what he wants. Today he has his Masters degree and will one day have his Doctorate degree.

My path may not be the same as his but he has told me many times how proud he is of me. We are both leaders and you can be too.

Just find your space. Find the place where you are true to who you are and where your inner soul can shine. This book is for all youths aspiring to be leaders.
Best of luck to you on your journey.

Checklist:
- Know yourself.
- Love yourself.
- Forgive yourself.
- Learn and move on.
- Love others as you love yourself.

* * * * *

No One Left Behind

A BFT is a Basic Battle Fitness test. The military uses this to see if their troops are physically fit to march long distances. As I was finishing my recruiting course, our BFT was 13.5 km in under 2.5 hours, fully equipped with our tack vests FFO (full fighting order) which consisted of all the military weaponry and protection and also included a rucksack that weighed 50 lbs.

Getting to the half-way point was the easy part. Turning around to complete the other half was the adventure.

The Youth Leadership Empowerment System

About 2 km into the return trip, one of the female troops felt as if she couldn't continue. I took her rifle and she unbuckled her helmet as she wanted to breathe easier. I advised her to drink some water and when she was finished, to buckle her helmet. I suggested we make a run for the front.

While running she stopped two times and said she couldn't do it. I kept encouraging her by reminding her that we made it this far so there was no point in quitting now.

When we finally got to the front, I handed her back her rifle. I made sure she was okay and then I went back to see if anyone else within the platoon needed help or encouragement.

~ ~ ~ ~ ~ ~ ~ ~ ~

"When the effective leader is finished with his work, the people say it happened naturally." — Lao Tzu

"The challenge of leadership is to be strong, but not rude; be kind, but not weak; be bold, but not bully; be thoughtful, but not lazy; be humble, but not timid; be proud, but not arrogant; have humor, but without folly."
— Jim Rohn

"A good leader will always ensure that no one is left behind." – Bryan Berkeley

~ ~ ~ ~ ~ ~ ~ ~ ~

Bryan Berkeley

Leaders look out for their team members.

There is a lot of rhetoric these days about leadership. Sometimes we can see straight through this talk, but other times it's difficult because of all the noise in our lives. Regardless of how you perceive it, you need to strive to look beyond the obvious.

This story is one that demonstrates a sincere love for your peers. A member of my unit was tired, discouraged, and disheartened by the training exercise. However, with my belief in her ability and my encouragement, she was able to make it to the front of the platoon.

Leaders will also go to the back of the line to ensure that no one is being left behind. You see that I went to the back to find her and then moved her to the front. Then I returned to the back to look for anyone else who might be in need of help.

I could very easily have focused on completing the training exercise by myself and let my team mate fend for herself. However, that would not by the gentlemanly thing to do. It would not be the military thing to do. It would not be the human thing to do.

You see, we are all connected to each other. In our military unit, if one member of the unit fails then we have all failed.

For the guys, do you think that the member of my unit felt a bit of admiration and respect for me? Of course she did. Do you think she knew that I cared for her and was a good friend to her in her time of need? Of course she did.

The Youth Leadership Empowerment System

Now there was nothing between me and the female member of my unit but on the battlefield, in the middle of a combat situation, I think she would be willing to defend me to the death because she saw my dedication to her.

That's the kind of loyalty we build up within our units in the army. That's the kind of friendships we need in our communities.

This lesson is an important one for guys today. You want girls who will be loyal to you to the end. Guys, you want a gal who will support you and satisfy you, that is, one who completes you. Well, to get a girl like that means that you must be a man who deserves such a woman.

You've got to be the type of guy who demonstrates loyalty to your girl. When a woman sees a guy willing to go an extra mile for her or make an extra effort for her, she really feels special.

We all feel special when someone takes a bit of extra effort for us. Young men and women should make every effort to develop this type of leadership characteristic within themselves.

Being a person who goes the extra distance for a friend can only give you a good reputation and make you more of a lovable person to others. If I help you and you help someone else, then our world becomes just a little bit better.

Checklist:

- Stretch yourself beyond your limit.
- Look out for your team members.
- Build true friendships that last.
- Act with honour.

* * * * *

The Youth Leadership Empowerment System

Monte Casino - All Jobs

This was my first job other than the military. Just like everyone else I really wanted to make a good impression, so I put in all that I could. As some people would say, I gave it my 100%. Lucky for me the boss was an ex-Major in the military so he hired me on the spot. Got my uniform and began to work that very same week.

Now, at Monte Casino the work habits and the line of work are entirely different from the military. I had to learn how to French-serve and how to wait a table. My boss always told me that anyone could be a waiter; give him a uniform and tell him/her to serve this table, but to wait a table is something totally different. And that was what I aimed for.

As the weeks went by I knew the entire staff and I couldn't really help anyone until the event had finished. Cleaning up, I finished all my tables with my partner and then helped every team around until the whole floor was clean. That was our job, serve and clean. Yet I stayed back and helped the next set of guys clear the floor of all tables and chairs.

When that was done, I didn't stop there. I knew the dish washers would be working hard for the next few hours trying to get all the dishes clean for the next day so I stayed and helped until all the work was finished.

I made sure every last dish was stacked away and the kitchen was cleaned before leaving and I wouldn't sign out until 7 the next morning. Go home and get some rest for the next day which began for me at 4:30pm, but I went early to help with the set up. Some days I would pull 14-hour shifts, but it helped out my coworkers a lot. They really appreciated my willingness to help out.

The Youth Leadership Empowerment System

~ ~ ~ ~ ~ ~ ~ ~

"I have three precious things which I hold fast and prize. The first is gentleness; the second is frugality; the third is humility, which keeps me from putting myself before others. Be gentle and you can be bold; be frugal and you can be liberal; avoid putting yourself before others and you can become a leader among men." - Lao-Tzu

"I suppose leadership at one time meant muscles; but today it means getting along with people." - Indira Gandhi

"A good leader will go out of their way to make things easier for the members of his team." – Bryan Berkeley

~ ~ ~ ~ ~ ~ ~ ~

Leaders lead by demonstrating excellence.

Talk about being a servant leader. That was exactly what I was doing in my role as an employee of Monte Casino. I was moving from one team to the next helping them finish their tasks. Even though I was not given an official leadership position in my job, I had earned the respect and admiration of my colleagues.

My actions answered the unspoken question, "How can I be of service?" I did not wait for someone to request my help. My eyes were always scanning the environment in search of opportunities to be of assistance. Do you think my colleagues liked me on the job? Yes, they all did. They were happy to have me working with them on their shift. In fact, they were happy because this young man was there to help make their lives a little bit easier.

With my military-trained body, I was fit and full of vitality. What they might have considered hard work, was warming up for me. I was able to work longer and harder without busting a sweat, so I was helping them while keeping myself running at a high potential. I was like the Energizer bunny.

My boss was also very happy that he hired me. He saw that I was a hard worker and a dedicated team member. He saw how I helped everyone and that I was liked by all the other staff. I was a good asset to his company. I was good for morale and good for getting the work done.

My attitude was one of taking pride in my work. Sometimes it seems that we, as young people, are losing that sense of pride in our work. We do stuff but it's almost like who cares, so we don't do our best.

An artist who paints a beautiful piece of art always signs their work. In fact, even a bad artist will sign their work or an art student will sign their work. Why? It is a way to be recognized for the work they have done. It is leaving their mark.

In everything we do in life, we are signing it with our character. If we do a job poorly, then it shows that we did not really care about that job. Did I care about my job at the Monte Casino? Of course, I did. Did I sign it with excellence? You bet I did.

This is the type of attitude young men and women should apply to whatever they are doing because everything you do is a reflection of you. So why not sign your life with your best!

Checklist:

- Practice your best signature.
- Live life with an attitude that says you're an asset.
- Be humble and diligent.
- Act with dedication.

* * * * *

Bryan Berkeley

The Bus Story

It was after midnight on a Friday and I was returning home from some military work. I got onto the bus to go home and stood in the middle of the bus. I noticed as we journeyed that a person who had too much to drink was making a scene on the bus. He was spewing rude and vulgar words to no one in particular on the bus.

He got up and went to the front of the bus to enquire of the driver and then returned to the back of the bus. As he passed me, he stammered up to me and attempted a salute. He then proceeded to his seat.

He began talking loudly to a young lady on the bus. He was touching her and she repeatedly told him to stop. He ignored her requests and continued on. When I observed that no one was coming to the aid of the young lady, I stood up and walked over to their position. I told him in a firm voice to leave the lady alone and have some self respect. This aggravated him and he stood up to engage me.

He raised his clenched fist in the air to strike me and paused. Then he pretended to strike but halted each time. This happened on two occasions. After the second time, I told him that if he were to hit me, I'd have to take him down and restrain him until the police came to arrest him.

To which he replied that I was lucky I was a military man; otherwise he would hit me. I ignored his comment and for the remainder of the ride I stood in between him and the young lady.

As I was getting off the bus at my stop, the young lady thanked me for coming to her rescue and two other passengers told me I that I had done the right thing.

~ ~ ~ ~ ~ ~ ~ ~

"The day soldiers stop bringing you their problems is the day you have stopped leading them. They have either lost confidence that you can help them or concluded that you do not care. Either case is a failure of leadership." - Colin Powell

"If I have the belief that I can do it, I will surely acquire the capacity to do it, even if I may not have it at the beginning." - Mahatma Gandhi

"A good leader will stand up for those in need of protection. " - Bryan Berkeley

Bryan Berkeley

~ ~ ~ ~ ~ ~ ~ ~

Leaders stand up for those who are weaker or in need.

As a young person, I am sure you have met a bully in your lifetime. Perhaps you were never picked on by the bully, but you have seen them picking on others. A bully is someone looking for attention in the wrong manner. If no one stands up to them, then they think they can get away with it.

That drunken man on the bus was being a bully to that lady on the bus. It was just like high school where no one wanted to get involved. Perhaps they were afraid of being beaten up by this bus bully.

Maybe some people were thinking that it was the driver's responsibility to ensure the safety of the female passenger. Who knows what everyone was thinking? What people thought doesn't matter because action was needed in that situation.

When I properly assessed the situation and recognized that after the female's repeated attempts to handle the situation were ineffective and recognizing that no one else was going to step in, I made the decision that had to be made. Step up and be the man.

I got in there and stood in the gap. I stood up for the woman and became her protector. She had Bryan Berkeley, Canadian Armed Forces soldier, come to her rescue. Do you think this lady was grateful? Of course, she was more than grateful. I came to her rescue in a situation where she was not making any progress. After my intervention, she was able to enjoy her bus ride in peace and comfort.

She was not bothered by the drunken man and she felt safe.

What about the drunken man on the bus, do you think he learned anything? He stood up to attempt to challenge me but still had the good sense not to do something stupid that could land him in jail.

You see, while he was making a fool of himself picking on the weaker lady, he felt he could continue to do it. When I stood up to him, he realized that his behaviour was not acceptable and that others felt so. When he knew he was in a no-win situation, he sat down quietly for the remainder of the trip.

The other passengers on the bus also learned that I am a young man with integrity, with honour, and I am willing to stand up for a woman in need of help in spite of the danger.

The bus driver was also happy that I intervened in that situation. Everyone should be able to feel safe in their daily travels. That night, I made the bus safer for everyone on board. I did this not out of a sense of wanting to be a hero. I did it because it was necessary to be done at that time.

Do you think that there are times in your life when you could be the hero? Of course there are. Everyone has moments in their life to shine. It's up to you to choose to act in those moments. The choice is always yours.

If you see the school bully attacking a student, if you cannot engage the bully, then go quickly and notify a teacher. Quick and decisive action may be needed to save the student being attacked. Your action may make the difference in that person's life that words cannot begin to describe.

Doing nothing is never the best option when you see others in need of help. There is an email that has seen circulating on the internet. I'm paraphrasing, but basically the gist of it is, they came for group 1 and I said nothing, then they came for group 2 and I said nothing. Finally they came for me and no one was left to say anything for me.

This email shows the essence of why we need to stick up for one another. This is why a leader needs to be the one to speak up for others. If we choose to be silent when our voices need to be raised, then we have done not only our neighbour, but also ourselves a great disservice.

Your voice, no matter how small a body it belongs to, can be a great signal in a time of need. As a leader to be, develop your voice to speak up. You should also develop the courage within yourself to stand up for what is right.

I'll tell you one other story my brother mentioned to me. At Ryerson University, there was this lady who ran one of the programs for students. My brother told me that this lady, his friend, mentioned to him that one time on Yonge Street she saw some police abusing a youth. She had observed the entire situation and noted that the boy's only wrong was being a bit mouthy.

The Youth Leadership Empowerment System

Well, when she saw what was going on, she crossed over the street and got into the police officer's face. She told him that she had seen his brutality and she wanted his badge number and business card. He started to raise his voice at her and she told him not to speak to her like that. The lady got the officer's information and gave the boy her card to call her if things got any worse.

The police didn't realize that this petite lady was a hardened youth counsellor who also had been around the police service and prison service. She knew the regulations and what the officers did that was overstepping their boundaries. She called the officer on it.

I tell you this story because it shows a tiny lady with a lot of knowledge could stand up to a police officer in defense of someone else. Now I must mention that I have a great respect for our honest and hardworking police officers. There may be some who are bullies in uniform, but their peers need to stand up to them and let them know it is not acceptable. We, like that lady, may need to stand up.

There is a principle called the Bystander Effect. It means that in a crowd of people, most people will assume that someone else will do the right thing and so no one does anything. You can see lots of videos of it by searching on YouTube.

There is a video of a security specialist simulating the kidnapping of a 7-year-old child. The child's mother was sitting in a van close by watching. There was also a police officer nearby in case things got out of control. Hidden cameras recorded the reaction of people as they passed by. Amazingly, as the girl shouted, "You're not my dad! Let me go!" people just continued to walk by. Some people looked back but just kept going.

This happened several times as they repeated the simulation. By then the mother of the girl was in tears as she realized that had it been a real situation, no one would help her daughter. Then as they were doing the simulation again, two black guys walked by with groceries and one was talking on a cell phone.

These two black guys heard the girl and turned to look. They continued watching and assessing the situation. Then, when they felt that it was a kidnapping, they both dropped their bags and ran to defend the girl and stop the simulated crime. At this point they were alerted to the police presence and the fact that it was a simulation.

Afterwards the men were interviewed and they said, at first they thought it was a girl misbehaving but when they kept looking, they said it looked like she was in real danger. So they just ran up to get involved.

The girl and her mother were both overjoyed that these two guys were heroes. They were willing to risk their lives to help out a little girl they thought was in danger. While everyone else suffered from the bystander effect as they walked past, something in the two men overcame this and they took action.

That is leadership!

You too, may have to stand up for a weaker person in need. When you do, know that you are doing your part to make this world a better place.

The Youth Leadership Empowerment System

Doing what is right is never a bad choice in my book.

Checklist:

- Always keep your eyes open to the situation around you.
- Stand up for a person in need of your help.
- Get others involved in stopping the injustice.
- Act with fortitude.

* * * * *

The Bus Fare Story

School had just finished and one of my friends was coming over to my place. Both of us got on the bus, paid our fare and went to the back of the bus. For some unknown reason, the bus went out of service. Everyone got off the bus and took a transfer to board another bus.

The bus stop was filled with people from that bus plus other students waiting for the bus to go home. The first bus came to a stop and it was packed. My friend and I decided to wait for the next one. Soon afterwards, the second bus came and it too, was packed with people. We decided to let the others get on and wait for the third bus.

Finally the third bus came and my friend and I went on

the bus. The bus driver began to argue with us about our transfers even though I explained that the other bus was out of service and what had happened. She said that high school students were always up to some schemes and insisted we pay again. I took out two tickets and paid for my friend and me.

As the bus passed by the one that went out of service, she stopped and asked the driver about our story. He verified that we were indeed telling the truth. When we got to the next stop the driver called me up to the front of the bus and gave me my two tickets back and apologized.

I thanked her and gently told her that she had just made a member of the Canadian Armed Forces look like an idiot and that she shouldn't think that all students are out to scam the public transit system.

There are those of us who uphold higher standards.

~ ~ ~ ~ ~ ~ ~ ~

"The ultimate measure of a man is not where he stands in moments of comfort, but where he stands at times of challenge and controversy." - Martin Luther King, Jr.

"True leadership must be for the benefit of the followers, not to enrich the leader." — John C. Maxwell

"Leaders keep their cool in any situation. " - Bryan Berkeley

~ ~ ~ ~ ~ ~ ~ ~

Leaders keep their cool.

Can you imagine being wrongfully accused even though you know that you are righteous? A certain man named Jesus of Nazareth experienced this.

This story I mentioned about the transit system highlights that sometimes people misjudge us in an undeserving manner. Had I been dressed in full military gear, she may have been more willing to believe me, but as I was dressed as a simple high school student, my word seemed unworthy.

At that point, I could have stood there and argued until I was blue in the face or made a commotion. But that was not the correct response in that scenario. Had I done more to aggravate the situation and cause tempers to flare, she might not have doubted her initial assessment and stopped to verify the situation. By remaining cool, I allowed her to remain cool also and to reevaluate the situation.

When she realized that she had made an error, she took steps to correct the mistake. Remember this point; a mistake is only a mistake if left uncorrected. At the time she corrected the error I chose to inject a life lesson for her benefit. That's why I mentioned being a member of the Canadian Armed Forces. It showed her that I held higher standards than ordinary civilians or even high school students.

Do you think she will remember that day?

Of course she will. I had made an impression on her twice

that day. First, by my quiet example of not arguing and becoming rude and by simply paying the fare, I showed her that I was not a typical high school student. The second time I made an impression on her was when she gave me back the tickets. I showed her that I represent the Canadian Armed Forces and that I could defend her and our country at any time. My standards are not those of typical high school students.

Now, I know of too many high school students who would lose their cool and begin cussing, swearing and causing a big commotion. What would that accomplish? It would allow you to vent your frustration, but more likely than not, it would create an unpleasant situation for everyone on the bus.

In the worst case, they could call the police for the student. That would mean too much time wasted in talk about why the student behaved that way instead of focusing on the driver's fault. Then it makes it harder for people to believe you.

If you think that you have been wronged, there are several ways to deal with it. The Toronto public transit has a number you can call to report any driver abuse or inappropriate action. If you ever feel that you've been wronged, then you need to simply note the date and time, the bus number and route and some details about the driver. Then you simply call it in.

The lesson here for a young person in a similar situation is to remain calm and allow reason to guide the conversation. If you believe you have been wronged, then there are means of redress at a later date. Don't blow your cool and make an already unpleasant situation worse. But be sure to get your point across.

Explain the situation clearly and give as much detail as you can. Then keep notes for yourself on the outcome. If your approach doesn't work, then try another approach.

I didn't give up, but after my words had done the talking, I let my character speak for itself. You should be able to do the same also.

Live your life to a higher standard. That way, you can always hold your head up high regardless of the situation.

Checklist:

- Always keep your cool in the situation around you.
- Use your words, then let your character speak for you.
- Conduct yourself with pride and etiquette.
- Tie in a life lesson whenever you can.

* * * * *

The Youth Leadership Empowerment System

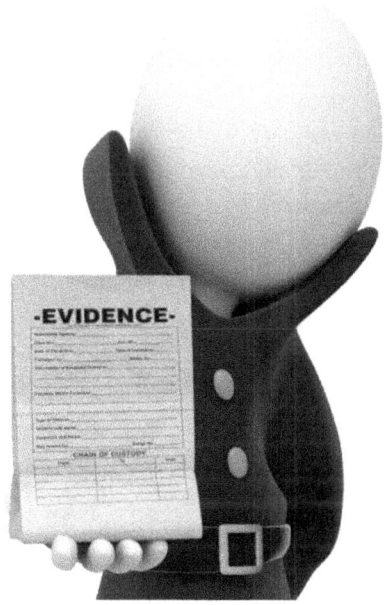

Changes on the Fly (BWW Kidnapping)

The BWW is the Basic Winter Warfare training exercise. It was a dark and blizzarding night. The temperature was -35 degrees Celsius. That night my section and I were out on midnight navigation exercises. As we got to the first checkpoint, we noticed a group of people with lots of lights on. We moved toward the position to investigate further and discovered it was another section out as well.

Our commanding officer radioed for clearance to engage the other section.

We began stalking them. They moved off the tree line, onto the road and we followed them. While maintaining a safe distance, we trailed them silently. When they stopped, we stopped. When they turned around to look behind them, we went prone. That is, made ourselves appear invisible to them in our winter gear camouflaged in the snow flurries. They walked right past us thinking we were part of a snow bank. When they turned to continue on their course, we continued to stalk them.

A few minutes later my commanding officer decided we should kidnap one of the members of the other section. As the junior man in my section, I was selected to engage in this exercise. I went down to the road to follow the other section while my section was still stalking them in the tree line. As I approached the target last man in their line, they stopped. I stopped.

He turned on his headlamp and looked behind him. I was about 10-12 ft. away from him. His lights hit my legs and my body but he didn't see me in my military gear. He switched off the light and continued marching forward. Almost instantly, I ran up behind him and grabbed him. With my hand over his mouth, I dragged him back into the tree line where my section stripped him of his equipment.

The section leader congratulated me on a flawless kidnapping.

For the remainder of the exercise he was considered dead. He could not talk to his section and had to follow orders from my section. We had him stand still in the middle of the road about 20-25 ft. behind his section. As his section leader did a count he realized he had lost a man. He halted the section and went to the back to investigate.

He looked in the distance to see his soldier. He raised his hand and signalled him to come up. No movement. He signalled again. Nothing. At this point he must have thought the soldier must have had some mental failure due to the weather. The section leader moved forward slowly while his section remained in position. The snow was falling heavily and visibility was minimal. As he got to within 10 ft. of the captured soldier, the soldier suddenly vanished. Gone.

We saw the section leader start to act with total disbelief. As the section leader got to within 5 ft. of us, we took off our hoods and headdresses and he saw floating heads in the road. At this point he understood that his section was being stalked.

We had made his missing soldier appear to vanish because we stood around him and our military camouflage hid him behind us.

Just then one of our soldiers came out with his rifle pointed at the section leader. He was captured.

We had accomplished our objectives.

~ ~ ~ ~ ~ ~ ~ ~

"Good attitudes among team players do not guarantee a team's success, but a bad attitude guarantees its failure. " – John C. Maxwell

"Effective negotiators know they can fulfill very challenging objectives when their "must-haves" or "like-to-haves" are grounded in realism and in what is achievable. " – Michael Benoliel

"The mission objectives can change on the fly. That is life. Youths must be able to adapt quickly to win. " – Bryan Berkeley

~ ~ ~ ~ ~ ~ ~ ~

Leaders know how to choose the right man for the right job when the mission changes.

In the story, we see illustrated many points of value to a young leader. First, the mission of our life can change on the fly. We must be willing to adapt. For example, as a child you might have wanted to be a doctor but when you got into high school, you realized that you hated sciences but loved mathematics.

At that point, you're not going to waste your time trying to be something you hate. You'd think about being a mathematician because you love math or strive for some other career that is math intensive.

They try to teach us about being adaptable in school by having us pick options. For example, you can select whether you want a soup or a sandwich for lunch. If sandwiches are finished, then your fallback is the soup.

In the story, we were supposed to be out on navigation training. This is pretty simple stuff. But in the middle of it, the opportunity arose to engage another unit out on night navigation manoeuvres. Our commanding officer turned a routine training exercise into a really cool training exercise by changing the mission objectives on the fly. And we all had a great time and loved him for it.

Sometimes in life we think we're going in one direction and all of a sudden we're thrown a curve ball and we have to take a detour. As a leader, you see it as an opportunity and an adventure and if you're quick, you can seize any advantages available to you on the new mission.

My commanding officer also knows how to choose the right man for the job. He knew that I was the junior man on the team and if I were captured, the loss would be minimal.

He also knew that I was a keener who demonstrated excellence in all my military exercises. He also knew that I showed leadership among my peers, so of course his selecting me to engage the other unit was a natural decision given his great leadership abilities.

Over time, as we use our leadership abilities, it becomes part of our nature and we can make the right decisions quickly and on the fly.

Checklist:

- Know your personal mission.
- Be positive as you go for it.
- If you find things changing on the fly, then use it as a positive opportunity.

- If you need help with the new mission, then don't be afraid to seek it.
- Be confident about yourself.

* * * * *

The Youth Leadership Empowerment System

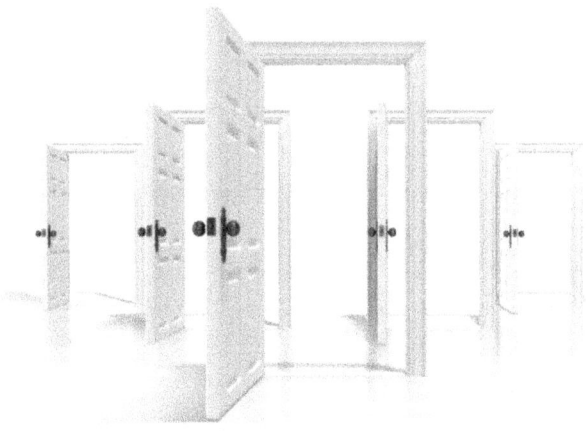

Leadership Knows No Boundaries

Youths today are in a time of unprecedented opportunity. We are also in a time of tremendous stress. Adults have managed to saturate every free space with information. Before the year 2000, our parents lived in an information age, but young people like me now live in an age of enlightenment.

The information must be combined with intuition, insight, charisma, and courage. In my time, I believe we will see more youths taking on the ranks of leadership. We will be giants in our own right.

Leadership is not exclusive to one group or one class of people. It is open to everyone. Any young person can become a leader if he or she wants to be one and is willing to do what it takes. No one can give leadership to anyone else. True leadership must originate from within us.

~ ~ ~ ~ ~ ~ ~ ~ ~

"People never improve unless they look to some standard or example higher and better than themselves. " - Tyron Edwards

"It's an old rule of effective armies that every officer rotates back into a troop command every few years. " - Peter F. Drucker

"I'm a leader, you're a leader, we're all leaders. " – Bryan Berkeley

~ ~ ~ ~ ~ ~ ~ ~ ~

In Stephen Covey's book, The Leader in Me, he mentions teachers, parents, and community leaders all wanting the same thing from young people. They wanted, "children to grow up to be responsible, caring, compassionate human beings who respected diversity and who knew how to do the right thing when faced with difficult decisions."

Here we have it. Adults want us to be good people. It's not about grades, though we should get good grades where we can. They want us to be great people so we can go on to make the world a better place. After all, when they are in their 70s, 80s and 90s they would like to be able to enjoy their retirement knowing the world is in good hands.

In December 2008, I gave a presentation in Brooklin,

The Youth Leadership Empowerment System

Ontario on leadership at a Christmas dinner.

The difference between a boss and leader is the boss says, "go" and the leader says, "let's go". A leader can be a leader even at the age of 5.

The acronym below represents the traits of a leader where each letter represents a different trait. I spent many hours turning the concept over in my mind to come up with this model. It is for youths and designed by me, a youth.

Leeway – A leader should be flexible. If a person wants to be a leader but they are too rigid and inflexible, then they become like a dictator. No one likes a dictator and soon that leader's authority will be hated and the leadership will be doomed to failure. At the same time, leadership is not a popularity contest. To like the popular person suggests that the popular person is very similar to the majority; thus he or she is one of the crowd and not suited to be a leader. A good leader will be different from the crowd but flexible in his or her approach to the crowd because this is necessary to be effective. Think of it like rock climbing and the leader is up front with five people connected with a line following behind. This leader needs to have the capability to give leeway because the others will experience the result of his or her poor choices. They are connected.

Education – In our society today, we need to have a higher level of education in order to be successful. And with leadership, like any other ability, there are certain fundamental principles that anyone can and must master in order to be a good leader. This is why I use the E in leader to represent education, as I believe it is one of the most important parts of leadership development.

Authority – Authority is also an important characteristic of a leader. Authority can come because a leader is very skilled and thus people respect their knowledge as being with authority. Authority can also come from a person's natural status within the society. For example, a mother has natural authority in the family when she tells her children what to do and what not to do.

She may not be an expert "child" so her authority and respect from her children is based on her natural status, that is, being a mother. Professionals like police officers, doctors, military personnel, teachers, and others get authority because of their years of training together with the circumstances they are currently in. So if a teacher walked into the emergency room of a hospital and began telling nurses to move this patient and prepare them for surgery, those instructions would not be followed. This is because the teacher's authority is only within the context of the classroom, not the emergency room.

During a flood when the police and the army are called out to help get people to safety and build sandbag barriers to lessen the damage, all civilians automatically listen to the instructions given. This is so because the training plus the circumstance are well suited to respect the authority of those professionals.

For a teenager among a group of your peers, it is difficult to be considered an authority if you have not accomplished anything for which your peers will respect you. And sometimes, the wrong person is given respect because of fear, for example, the bully in school. Yet, the kid who stands up will get respect from his peers.

The Youth Leadership Empowerment System

Different – Every leader is different in his or her own way. Any person in a leadership position will demonstrate a type of leadership that is part of their brand and their identity. Basically, think of it like cell phone companies. They all basically sell the same product, yet each company will have different perks and incentives in order to get people to buy into their brand. Once people buy into the particular brand, then the company will do other things to try to build loyalty to that brand. A leader is a brand. Otherwise, why would anyone see something different or better in that person that makes them want to follow that person?

If you want to develop leadership in yourself, then you must not be afraid of being different. You must embrace your being different but at the same time, your being different should not be a barrier, but more of a motivation for others among your peers to try to be like you.

Exclusive – The end result of the work that the leader does with his or her followers is unique. If the leader is just a cookie-cutter, same-as-everyone-else leader, then those who follow that leader will not have a chance to change. The end result would be no different for the followers. However if the leader is different and has a clear objective that at the end of the exercise, his or her followers will become unique and better people because of his or her leadership, then the result is exclusive.

Ready –Good leaders must be always in a state of readiness for anything that may occur within their environment. The unexpected always happens and being a good leader means being able to understand how to react to those unplanned events in a way that allows for benefit for his or her followers. Using my military training as an example, in my courses, we are taught to be prepared for the unexpected and we are trained to react a certain way. Why is this? It is because when such a situation arises, it will become like instinct for us to act because at the moment, there may not be enough time to think about what to do.

As a leader, you want to be able to give yourself as much training as possible in different scenarios so that you are able to reach a good solution instantly and without hesitating, should the need arise. This could be if you are a student leader in the classroom. Let's suppose your class goes on a field trip, and you happened to do a First Aid and CPR class and were certified the year before. Now if someone gets hurt, you will immediately jump into action because you are trained to react correctly.

The knowledge allows for greater and more effective readiness. So learn as much as you can and always be ready because you are a leader.

This leadership concept was a foundation of knowledge that I applied to myself for a few years. I defined these principles because they are simple to comprehend for very young people. Kids and teens will get it. On my website, I go into more advanced leadership training that I have learnt since being in the military and taking several leadership courses. You can find out more about the program on my website at
http://youthleadershipempowermentsystem.com

In this chapter we covered the basic principles of a leader

from a youth's perspective. Leadership is not as hard as some people believe. If you want to be different, want to be prepared, want to help those around you, you have the potential already to become a leader.

Checklist:

- Take time to develop your core values that are unique.
- Describe yourself using the acronym L.E.A.D.E.R
- How can you improve yourself in each LEADER area?
- Outline two things you will do this year to help yourself.
- Imagine yourself as a great leader.

* * * * *

Making Yourself Job Ready

Towards the end of my final year of high school, we were invited to go to an employment fair.

Employment fairs are great for students looking for work. This experience was like many other great experiences in my life. When I arrived, my teacher was immediately impressed with my appearance. While all the other high school students were in jeans, ripped clothes, or dressed way too casually, I was wearing a shirt and tie along with black pants and dress shoes. You can imagine that I stood out from everyone else who dressed unprepared for the occasion.

Before going into the employment fair, we had the opportunity to have our resumes reviewed by a panel of qualified reviewers. I gave each of them a copy of my resume. They were speechless. After a long silence, they questioned me about whether I had written my resume. I told them that the resume accurately reflects my experience and that I do believe it is okay to hire someone to write a resume.

They were impressed by both the quality of the resume and my wisdom in making sure it was a professional document. One of the panelists called over a member of the Toronto Catholic District School Board to look at my resume. She asked me for a copy for herself. She uses sample resumes to show students what is the right way to prepare a resume. I'm sure she was going to use mine.

After wowing the panelists, I proceeded to the exhibit area where the employers were waiting.

I walked over to the booth where they were recruiting security guards. This was no ordinary security job, however. Most security guards operate under a watch-and-report mandate. This means that they rarely engage and neutralize situations. The booth I was at happened to be one that actually engages and neutralizes situations.

Good work for a military-trained teenager. We spoke and I gave the recruiter one of my resumes. He was visibly impressed. About five minutes after I left the booth, he came up to me at another booth and he asked if he could have four more copies of my resume. He said he'd put them into all the different departments for me and I would definitely get a call within a week. I gave him my resumes and thanked him.

As I walked around talking with recruiters and handing out resumes, I had three more experiences similar to the one at the security booth. People wanted my resume and wanted extra copies for submission to other departments in their organizations.

One lady from another booth even came up to me and told me that another recruiter told her that she must get my resume. I asked her why. She explained to me that I should just look around. I was the most professional looking teenager there. I politely told her that her words were kind but unfair to the other youths. She smiled and commented that even my words in response to her demonstrated maturity.

I thanked her again and gave her a resume. When she saw that I had actual work experience she was again impressed. We parted ways and she said she would be in touch.

After giving out more resumes and speaking with a few more recruiters I headed home satisfied that I had done my task well and had accomplished my mission at the event.

~ ~ ~ ~ ~ ~ ~ ~ ~

"My biggest difficulty in asking people to serve is that they are painfully aware of their lack of experience and lack of preparation. If we can provide them with that, they're eager to learn. " - Father Leo Bartel, Catholic Diocese of Rockford

"The purpose of a team is to make the strengths of each

person effective, and his or her weaknesses irrelevant. " - Peter F. Drucker

"People expect young people to behave immaturely or to be unprepared. Just by taking the time to look business-like and having a professional resume, you will stand out from the rest. If you know your environment and you know yourself, you can get the victory. " - Bryan Berkeley

~ ~ ~ ~ ~ ~ ~ ~

Leaders stand out like giants among pygmies.

Employers want to have employees who can perform at optimum potential. Covey (2008) mentions a list of ten traits that employers are looking for in students who will enter the workforce which include:

- Communication Skills
- Honesty / Integrity
- Teamwork Skills
- Interpersonal Skills
- Self Motivation / Initiative
- Strong Work Ethic
- Analytical Skills
- Technology Skills
- Organizational Skills
- Creative Minds

Did you see the point on high grades? No, it didn't make the list. Most employers can teach you what you need to know about their business, but they can't teach you the fundamentals above.

If we look at the story I illustrated earlier about the employment fair, you'll see that I conveyed most of these points to the recruiters at the fair. They got buzz going and they were impressed and told other recruiters about me. That led to more buzz about this great candidate.

Here's a breakdown of the situation.

1. I talked to the employers with respect and genuine interest in their organizations. I was clear in my communications and listened well. (☐ Good Communication Skills)
2. I told each of them my career plans and that I would be on a military training over the summer so I'd only be available for work upon my return. They liked my honesty with them. The lady I mentioned above who complimented me was impressed with my integrity by my standing up for my peers who were not prepared for the occasion. (☐ Honesty / Integrity)
3. My resume highlighted my combat training and exercises with my unit. In the military we have to function effectively as a team. (☐ Teamwork Skills)
4. I built good rapport with each recruiter within a few minutes of speaking to them. (☐ Good Interpersonal Skills)
5. My resume highlighted the fact that I've always been a go-getter. Working part-time jobs, volunteering and going after what I want. (☐ Self Motivation / Initiative)
6. My resume highlighted the part-time jobs I've held. I also spoke of my willingness to work. Added to that was the fact that a couple of my co-workers happened to be at the employment fair as the Monte Casino Banquet Hall, one of my

employers, was the venue for the fair. (☐ Strong Work Ethics)

7. The analytical and technology skills are based on the type of job I was interested in. Different jobs require different levels of these skill sets. I attempted to choose jobs where my strengths would be a good match. (☐ Analytic/Technology Skills)

8. My organizational skills were aptly demonstrated by my dress, my well crafted resume and my bringing enough paper copies. My business attire made me stand out from my peers. The school board wanted us to bring our resumes on a USB drive, however I noticed that not many of the recruiters came prepared with laptops. Thus if a student came only with the USB, they'd be out of luck. (☐ Good Organizational Skills)

9. I have tried over the years to nurture my creativity. The military training I received also allowed me to learn strategic and tactical knowledge from those more experienced than myself. Then I try to enhance the learning with my imagination and playing scenarios over in my mind. This shows in the way I anticipated what was expected at the employment fair. (☐ Demonstrated Creative Mind)

Can any average high school student demonstrate the above skills to recruiters and potential employers? Yes, absolutely. If you play team sports, you demonstrate teamwork. If you volunteer and are consistent in your punctuality, you can demonstrate a strong work ethic. If you are always the centre of attention at parties or gatherings, you can demonstrate good interpersonal skills.

You need to find a way to effectively describe your skills and abilities. It does require that you take some time to know yourself and that you put things down on paper. My resume was actually prepared the semester prior to the employment fair. I then only needed to update it periodically.

With the completion of this book, I'll be able to update my resume again. I will also have an expanded skill set.

I was hired by one of the organizations and got certified for personal security in Ontario. It's another funny story. While attending the classes to get the license, our instructor covered what to do when a bomb threat is in a room. I noticed a few differences between what he was teaching and what I had learned in the military. So I got to share my knowledge about the safe way to get clear of that situation.

However, I got my dream job which is full-time in the Canadian Armed Forces. It is the environment for me for this time in my life.

The important lesson here is to be prepared for your situation. I can't say that it is all me. I have had the encouragement and support of my family members. My mom encouraged me to get a job and my brother encouraged me to get a good resume. A youth leader knows when to listen to good advice and when to act on it.

The Youth Leadership Empowerment System

Checklist:

- Write Down Your Skills and Abilities.
- Create a Resume.
- Have a trusted source review it.
- Revise and review until good.
- Submit it to organizations that match your skills and desired area of learning.
- Be confident about yourself.

* * * * *

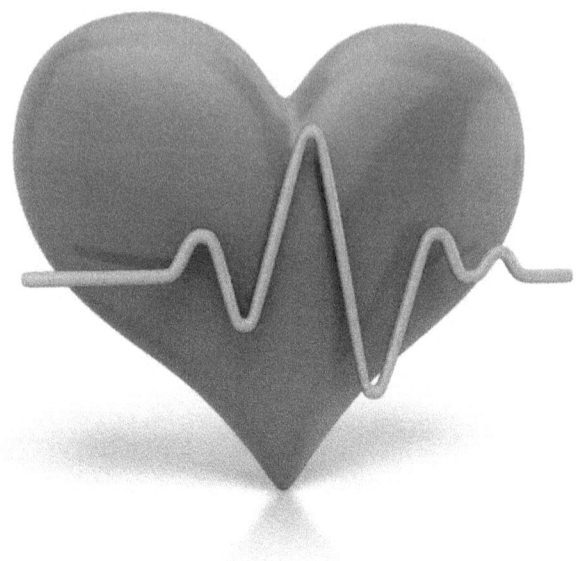

Diet and Health

Contributed by Jenny Berkeley, RN, Health Educator, Kindle Author

When I heard that Bryan was writing a book on leadership for young people, I was delighted by the motivation of this young man. I am even more delighted and honoured by the fact that I am able to contribute a chapter on health for young people in Bryan's great work. You see, too many young people don't get proper education in what could be called their natural intuition about food and health.

Though many parents have the best intentions, it is an unfortunate side-effect of this fast-paced lifestyle that we lead in this modern-day society that has seen the children deprived of the essential knowledge for good health.

I have written extensively on the topic of good health from my personal experience of over 20 years plus my education in healthy living and living foods nutrition. In one chapter I cannot possibly cover the wide range of information that I would like to share with you. However I will do my best to give you a few gems of information that you can use in your daily living.

~ ~ ~ ~ ~ ~ ~ ~

"Leaders need to be optimists. Their vision is beyond the present." - Rudy Giuliani

"The most important single influence in the life of a person is another person… who is worthy of emulation."
– Paul D. Shafer

"Don't believe that you know everything. Never be ashamed to seek the help of those who have the knowledge you need to empower yourself. " – Bryan Berkeley

~ ~ ~ ~ ~ ~ ~ ~

In the spirit in which Bryan's book is written, we will start out by breaking some of the myths that you as a young person would have heard over the years. But before we do that, let's look at the definition of insanity. "Insanity" is doing the same thing over and over and expecting to get a different result each time. Or to put it another way, it is trying to bang your head against the wall and each time hoping the wall will move.

Myth #1: Our Parents Knew All About Good Health

Let's look at myth number one. Some young people develop the idea that parents know best about good health. Some young people assume that because their parents live in a certain way that it is in their best interest to live that same way. I'd like to ask you to question your previous beliefs. I'm not saying that your parents were wrong, necessarily. What I am saying is that you need to evaluate the things that you have been taught for yourself and arrive at the correct conclusion. This is a sign of both maturity and wisdom.

Now, remember I mentioned earlier the definition of insanity. In the hospital environment, the doctor will often ask the patient for their family medical history. What do you think this family medical history can sometimes be an indication of? If your grandmother suffered with diabetes and your parents suffered with diabetes and you are currently a borderline diabetic, then what logical conclusion can you draw? You could say that your family has a genetic predisposition toward diabetes or you could say diabetes runs in your family. I like to think of one doctor who said he's Italian and some would say diabetes runs in the family, high blood pressure runs in the family, and high cholesterol runs in the family, but he says what really runs in the family is spaghetti and meatballs, pasta dishes filled with cheese and other such dishes.

What I am trying to tell you, the young reader in this section, is if your grandmother or grandfather had diabetes, high blood pressure, cholesterol or any other lifestyle-related disease and if your parents also suffered from these diseases, then you should consider that what they are doing in terms of diet and health is not working. Therefore if you continue to do what they did, then you will by definition, be undertaking an exercise in insanity if you want a different result. The logical and sane thing for you to do is change your lifestyle to get the different result.

Myth #2: I Can Eat Anything I Want And Get Away With It.

You know that there are some young people who have the uncanny ability to eat and eat anything and yet seem to never have any body fat. Then there are other young people who appear to simply have to inhale the smell of a fatty food and they seem to gain weight. Well, here's the crux of the matter. You can eat whatever you want, but you can never avoid the consequences of your eating choices.

What do I mean here? I mean that eating a certain way while you are young seems to go unnoticed because your body is able to compensate at a rapid rate. Even if you exercise, but still eat junk you will experience the results of your choices sooner or later. I'll give you the example of a friend of mine whose name is Paul Nison. He was a very athletic young man and very intelligent, however he ate the standard unhealthy diet that most young people eat. Then suddenly and without warning, he came down with inflammatory bowel syndrome (IBS). It was one of the most painful and unpleasant experiences of his life.

Each day he got sicker and sicker while searching for a cure. The doctors told him his disease was incurable. But he never gave up hope. That was the beginning of a journey that led him to be the man that he is today. Eventually he was cured of his IBS by changing his diet and lifestyle.

My husband has a story about a schoolmate of his at Ryerson University. She was a talented young lady; she was involved in numerous activities in the school; she was also liked by her friends. Then within a couple of years of graduating she also became very ill. She had issues with the stomach. This sickness was the catalyst which led her to change her life and eating habits. Now you may probably know her as a popular writer and vegan diet advocate.

My dear young people, you need to understand that your body is precious and you need to take care of it and that includes minding what you put into your mouth.

Myth #3: One Bowel Movement Per Day Or Every Other Day Is Normal.

Let me tell you right now that if you eat three times a day and you have one or less bowel movements for the day, then you are experiencing constipation. One time I remember being with some people who were discussing constipation and one teenage girl thought that not having a bowel movement every day was normal. She was quite surprised to learn that she should be eliminating at least once per day and ideally one movement for every meal consumed.

If you are not in the habit of eliminating every day, then you need to reform your diet, your exercise routine, and perhaps even your posture on the toilet. I've written about this in my books and given lectures on this, so I won't go into it here but I encourage you to get my books and read up on it yourself.

Healthy Habits of a Young Leader

Now that I have covered three myths associated with poor lifestyle, I'll give you a few pointers that you need to know in order to optimize your youth and prepare your young minds for leadership. If you will nourish your mind and body to be healthy and strong, you unlock a world of potential. Here are a few positive habits you should develop in your life.

Habit #1: Eating for Strength and Not for Gluttony

Young people are being taught improper eating habits from a very young age. I have noticed, for example, in elementary school children have breakfast by 7:30 or 8:00 in the morning, then they have snack time at 10:00 or 10:30, followed by lunch at noon, snack time at 2 or 3 and lastly dinner by 7 pm. The children have spent the entire day eating. The digestive systems have not had sufficient time to rest. Ideally one should wait 4 to 5 hours before having their next meal. And by the way, a snack is considered a meal because your body cannot tell the difference between a snack and a meal.

Food is food.

As a general rule, 2 to 3 meals per day should be sufficient to satisfy your body's dietary needs. You do not need to eat more than this and you do not need to snack between meals. Also when you are eating, do not eat until you are completely stuffed, but instead leave a little breathing room for your stomach muscles to do the job of digesting.

Habit #2: Drinking Water in the Proper Amount and Time

It was Dr. Batmanghelidj who said, "waiting until you are thirsty to drink water is allowing yourself to die a slow and painful death." You see, we lose water every day. We lose water through the act of breathing. You can see that on a cold winter day as your breath leaves your body. We also lose water through perspiration on a daily basis. And then we lose water via the process of urination.
So what is the proper amount of water to drink per day and when is the best time to drink water?

Everyone's body is different and therefore a one-size-fits-all approach to drinking water will not work for everyone. Athletes also require more water than ordinary, sedentary people. Dr. David Carpenter recommends that you drink half your body weight in ounces every 24 hours as a minimum water replacement level. For example, if you weigh 100 lbs, then you should drink 50 ounces of water per day as a start. You can drink more water if you exercise more, lead a more active lifestyle, or live in a hot climate.

So now that we've covered how much water to drink, we should look at when is the best time to drink.

Tip 1: Never drink water or any liquids with your meals.

This dilutes your stomach acid and messes up your digestion process.

Tip 2: Drink water 30 minutes to 1 hour before your meal. You can drink a cup or two of lukewarm water 30 minutes to 1 hour before your meal. The water will have time to leave your stomach before you eat.

Tip 3: Drink 2 to 3 cups of lukewarm water when you wake up in the morning.

Habit #3: Proper Bowel Movements (Pooping)

You need to create a healthy habit of pooping daily. If you already have a poor routine of going to the toilet, then you may have to potty train yourself all over again. Don't laugh too much because while it sounds laughable now, it's not funny to be a 30 or 40-year-old diagnosed with colon cancer.

Proper colon health in as important in your youth as it is in your old age. If you want to have more health, vitality and fun out of your life, then you have to take care of your colon. This means training yourself to have regular bowel movements.

I actually teach an entire course on colon health, so I won't go into all the details here. However, I'll help you figure out one method to train yourself to have better bowel movements.

Here are a few simple tips for training yourself to have better bowel movements.

Tip 1: Follow the water drinking protocol mentioned earlier. Also, drinking more water first thing in the morning when you wake up is good.

Tip 2: Don't hold in the poop and wait for another time. When you begin to feel the urge to poop, then immediately go to the nearest toilet. Some people put it off for whatever reason. Delaying it causes the body to extract more moisture from it and makes it harder. If you wait too long, you'll have a hard painful rock to pass which increases risks of tearing your anus.

Tip 3: Sit on the toilet every morning. Make a routine of attempting to poop every morning. Don't force it. Just assume the position and let it come out. Do this every day. As time goes by, your body will realize that you poop in the morning and it will signal you that it is ready to poop.

Finally, good health is everyone's responsibility. As a budding leader, it is your responsibility to give yourself a strong mind and body. Feed your body with the best nutrients in the right time, and let your body be strong for leading others.

I publish a holistic health magazine in Toronto that is filled with healthy lifestyle information called EternityWatch magazine. It is also available online at www.eternitywatchmagazine.com My personal website also contains lots of health tips, review of things in the news, recipes and more. You can see them on my site at www.eating4eternity.org

The Youth Leadership Empowerment System

Peace and be well. - Jenny Berkeley

* * * * *

Money Smarts For Youth

Contributed by Vaughn Berkeley, MBA

Youths today need a basic financial plan to help them achieve a measure of financial success. What is financial success? Is it being rich? Is it being able to have the money you need so that you are never lacking? Is it having more money when the month finishes?

Financial success means different things for different people and cultures.

The Youth Leadership Empowerment System

In today's Western culture, it appears that young people are conditioned to think that financial success is in the amount of things that a person can buy. That's why music videos are shot in mansions or very often depict scenes of jets, of lavish wealth, or of lots of money.

The success of Pinterest is another great example of "desire marketing." The site presents images of items that people may want to have in their lives. These can be nice clothes, nice body, nice houses, nice cars, or whatever the heart can desire. Thus people are constantly bombarded with marketing images since virtually all images are marketing something.

~ ~ ~ ~ ~ ~ ~ ~

"We need to teach the next generation of children from day one that they are responsible for their lives." – Elisabeth Kubler-Ross

"Life is just an endless chain of judgements… The more imperfect our judgement, the less perfect our success." – Paul D. Shafer

"Youths need money and youths need experience. By working daily, gaining experience, and thinking of new ways to make money, a youth can build a better and brighter future. " – Bryan Berkeley

~ ~ ~ ~ ~ ~ ~ ~

I am honoured to be able to be a guest contributor to a chapter in Bryan's book for youths. Indeed, learning financial abilities is important to all people. I'll cover just four myths that are drilled into youth and offer you four ideas for a different reality.

Myth #1: You Need A University Or College Degree In Order To Make Money.

This is a myth put forth to all people in order to keep the idea of a university or college education as being an "elite" venture. Many people have been making money for centuries without a university education. In fact, in many cases, getting a university education conditions you to become a lifelong servant to the profession you selected at the onset of your education.

There are many university students who graduate with 30K or 40K or even $100,000 in student debt and don't make enough money to cover the debt and have a great life. There is a great documentary that talks about the false claims of higher education being essential. In it, Dr. Pamela Bacon, DDS, talks about her personal experience with higher education and how it ruined her life. She says that she would have been better off if she went to work at McDonald's.

The College Conspiracy is one must-watch video on Youtube:
 http://www.youtube.com/watch?v=xl7R8xIxzKI

And there are many more stories about doctors struggling with massive debt after getting their over-priced education. On one Toronto radio station in September of 2012, I heard a girlfriend of a doctor call in to the radio show. She said she was concerned that her heart surgeon boyfriend was trying to brush her off or something. He had told her that he was taking a part-time job as a security guard to get extra money.

When the show called him, it turned out that he was taking the part-time job as a security guard because he could not afford to keep spending all his money on his girlfriend. Now the entire listening audience of Toronto heard about this doctor freelancing as a security guard to earn more money. So being a high-paid heart surgeon still does not provide a person with enough money to live lavishly.

A higher education may be useful for very specialized persons in professions that require this type of training, but for the vast majority, a higher education is almost useless. The transferable skills that a youth learns outside of the school system is what will empower the youth to a better future.

Now I am not saying that college or university is not important. I am saying that if you cannot afford a university or college degree, don't let that stop you from going out and making something better for yourself in the world as an entrepreneur. Resourcefulness is not learnt in college or university. It is part of your spirit from birth.

Myth #2: You Need A Business Plan In Order To Start A Business.

This is the statement made with almost religious fervour at most levels of society. People are somehow led to believe that they need a business plan in order to have a business. That is false. While a business plan shows that you have given a lot of thought to your business, it does not guarantee success in any business.

The real purpose of a business plan is to allow you to borrow money from a lender. And in order to get access to that money you have to lay out your plan with all your secret suppliers, distribution channels, and other competitive intelligence information in the hopes that you will be loaned money for your business venture.

So if you are not intending to borrow money to start a business, then you don't need a detailed business plan at all. What you need is a five-year goal, an annual goal, a quarterly goal, and a monthly goal with respect to your sales, expenses, and profit. Your ability to watch your spending while making more money is the key.

Myth #3: You Need To Borrow Money To Make Money.

This is a myth that is very beneficial to the money-lending industry. If you have no business plan, you won't have access to borrowed money. When you borrow money, you still have to work hard, and it is your sweat and effort that builds the business.

Borrowing money for a business just makes your mistake more dangerous. For example, if you invested $1000 in your summer business from your savings, and your business goes under after the summer, then you have lost only your $1000 investment. This is sad, but you are back at zero and can build again. However, if you borrow $1000 for your summer business and it fails, you are at a dire loss. If the interest is 20%, you still owe $1200 even after your business has failed. You cannot walk away.

In India, cotton farmers borrowed money to buy genetically modified seeds to plant. They hoped to have huge harvests so they could sell the cotton, pay back the loans, and make a lot of money for themselves. Instead they got crop failures. And it was so bad that over 250,000 farmers have killed themselves in India due to this horrible situation.

The only winners when you borrow money are the money-lenders who benefit from your labour for doing absolutely nothing. They do this by charging interest on the loans.

Myth #4: If You Don't Conform To Others, Then You Are A Failure.

This is another lie told to youth. This lie is woven across many areas. Sometimes the lie is if you don't get into a good school, you will be a failure. Sometimes it is if you don't get a good job, you will be a failure. Other times it is if you don't marry the right person, you will be a failure. And the biggest lie is if you don't fit into the consumerism model, then you will be a big failure.

This is a lie to keep you enslaved to the never-ending cycle of buy-spend, buy-spend, buy-spend. But as leaders or potential leaders, you have to be willing to step outside of the box built for average people in society.

For some, making $1 million a year may be sufficient for them. For others, it is making $3,000 a year. For one person it may be being a PhD, for another it may be being an expert tradesperson that makes them feel happy.

Don't sacrifice your happiness to fit into another person's mold of what you should be. Find the path in life that brings you the most joy and adds the most value to the world. This is your true path and will make you a true success.

~ ~ ~ ~ ~ ~ ~ ~ ~

Now that we have shed the light on four myths that are taught to youth in order to constrain and restrict their world, I'll share with you four truths that you need to understand in order to help you move ahead with a sense of financial comfort.

Truth #1: Use the Apple Seed Principle of Economics

When a farmer plants an apple seed in the ground, he cares for the young plant. Then once the plant is grown, the tree will produce many apples which the farmer can sell. Too many people do not plant any seeds to produce fruits that will lead to financial security in later years. They simply live their lives from paycheque to paycheque and never take the chance to invest their money into a venture that will succeed.

If you want to be financially successful in your later years, begin by planting seeds today that will give you financial fruit in 5, 10, or 20 years. Plant more and more of those types of seeds in your life and you will get to a very successful financial future over time.

One example of this is purchasing a small piece of land when you are young. Though the land may seem of limited value, it will increase in value by the time you are ready to sell it in 5, 10, or 20 years. And if you have not borrowed any money to get the land, then all the increased value is yours at the time of your sale.

Truth #2: The Worldwide System of Interest Has Inflated All Prices

The system of interest currently used in the world is in fact usury. If we look back to 150 years ago, usury was charging interest on anything. Today, society is led to believe that charging reasonable interest rates is acceptable while interest rates that are too high is usury. All interest higher than 0% is usury according to the heavenly principle.

I saw a credit card statement that showed a balance of just over $500 owing. According to the statement, by making only the minimum monthly payment, it would take roughly 11 years to pay off the debt. Really?? Eleven years to pay off a debt of just over $500. This is one area where the working class lose their money.

There are three areas in total where money is stolen from the working class primarily. These are:
- Interest Rates on Credit Cards, Loans, and Mortgages
- Inflation by Interest Charges Along the Supply Chain
- Interest Charges on the Money Supply Causing Income Taxes

I'll explain each of them briefly here but to learn more you will need to read more books on the money supply, the banking system and on interest.

Interest Rates on Credit Cards, Loans, Student Loans, and Mortgages

I have touched on the credit card debt with the example above. When I was attending university, I noticed every semester the credit card companies were on campus offering students a free gift for signing up to get their credit card. They offered the credit card as a solution for cash-strapped students. The student could just pull out the credit card to pay for items and then pay later. The problem with that is that it becomes easy for the student to mismanage their spending habit and accumulate a massive amount of credit card debt. I know of one university student who accumulated several thousand dollars in debt while in the first couple of years of university. This made life difficult for the student upon graduating because of being stuck trying to pay off the debt.

Another student I know of ended up with a debt of over $70,000 with interest on her student loan. It took many years to pay down that debt and she lived very poorly and denied herself of many things because she didn't want that debt hanging over her head.

But it is not just students in college or university under the burden of debt. As you join the workforce, you may want furniture, clothes, a car, and other items to make day-to-day living better. Many times average people will go into debt by using their credit card or a line of credit or even the store credit package. This means that you can have the item now but you pay sometimes double the price for it later on.

The Youth Leadership Empowerment System

You are probably too young, but there was a concept known as layaway. This is where a person who wanted something would talk to the store owner and pay a little bit of money every week until the item was paid for. Then they could have the item. There was no interest charge and as the purchaser, you simply had to wait until you paid for the item before you could have it.

Credit has turned this model on its head and resulted in you paying a higher price. The seller also pays a higher price because of the service charges demanded by the credit card company. So the seller and the customer are paying money for an intermediary where none is needed.

Mortgages are another lending tool which have manipulated the market. Access to easy loans has allowed home sellers to be greedy and ask for higher prices each year. Since 2009, in America, many homes have been said to be well below market value. Actually, they've been properly priced. Housing should not have been so expensive in the first place. If you are thinking of buying a property, always look for the true value of the property and get the lowest mortgage or pay cash for your home and avoid the mortgage if you can.

Loans for cars have also allowed automakers to sell their cars much higher than is really necessary for the public good. When you buy a car, the minute you drive it off the lot it loses 25% to 50% of its value. Suppose you buy a $30,000 car by getting a car loan. The minute you drive off with your car, it is worth $22,500 or less. But you will still be stuck with the $30,000 loan plus interest. That is comparable to burning your money in a pit. Never buy a new car. A well maintained, used car that you can afford will serve you much better and give you peace of mind.

Interest on the Supply Chain

The lending institutions make money by charging interest all along the supply chain and so at each step the price is inflated to allow the seller to make a reasonable profit. This means that as the consumer, you are always paying a higher price.

Let's take a simple hypothetical example to illustrate the point. Ruby's cotton pants sells some of the finest pants around. Ruby sells them for $200 a pair. How did Ruby's cotton pants get to be so expensive? Let's see.

The cotton farmer in India had to borrow huge loans from the bank at a high interest rate in order to buy the cotton seeds to plant. From the price he sets for his cotton, 50% goes to the banks and he keeps 50%. Let's suppose that it works out to $20 as the cost for cotton for the pants. Then the cotton manufacturer purchases the cotton from the farmer and converts it to cotton cloth and thread. But the factory borrowed money to buy new equipment and repair its building. So it has to charge a higher price to pay back the loan and interest. Let's suppose this adds another $50 on to the price of the pants. The importer bringing the cotton to Canada also borrowed money to do the business. So this adds another $40 onto the price of the pants. Finally Ruby gets the cloth and thread and makes the high quality pants. Sadly, Ruby also borrowed money for her business and so, she too has to repay the money and interest. Let's suppose that $30 of the cost goes to pay the loan.

The Youth Leadership Empowerment System

Cost of pants = $200 which is broken down:
- $10 for farmer and $10 for bank
- $25 for manufacturer and $25 for the bank
- $20 for importer and $20 for the bank
- $60 for Ruby and $30 for the bank.

The price of the pants' creation is $115, plus the cost of interest - $85. This simple example illustrates the concept about what is taking place all across society.

If you cut out all the bank lending from the entire process, the price of the product would be a lot cheaper for you to buy. This happens with almost everything that is produced in society today with the exception of a few items.

Interest on the Money Supply Causing Taxes

The last point you need to be aware of is the concept of the government borrowing money from the central bank in order to repay it with interest which does not exist. It's like a never-ending cycle of interest that can never be eliminated by playing the game.

For simplicity, we'll use round numbers again. Suppose the government wants to print $1 billion. The central bank will agree to lend the government $1 billion at $200 million interest.

With every loan, there must be some form of collateral in case the borrower does not pay. So what do you think is the government's collateral? It is the citizens of the country. They are the collateral for the loan. Every person born into the society is thus born into debt bondage as surety for this loan.

Back to the loan. The $1 billion gets printed and the nice new notes are used by the government to run its programs and pay salaries. Taxes are collected from the people in order to repay the loan. But there is a big problem. The government does not collect $1 billion in taxes. Plus it owes $1 billion and $200 million to the bank. So it goes back to the bank the next year and asks for another loan to run its programs, pay salaries, and cover the interest on the first loan.

In year two, the government asks for $1.5 billion which will cost an additional $300 million in interest.

Year 1: Loan Amount: $1 billion, Interest: $200 million.
Year 2: Loan Amount: $1.5 billion, Interest: $300 million, Partial loan payment from year 1: $500 million.

The total now owed by the government is ($1.2 billion + $1.8 billion) - $0.5 billion = $2.5 billion.

And using this cycle, the debt never can and never will be repaid. Even if everyone in the country gave up all their money to the government, the loan still cannot be repaid because the interest part is never printed.

Income taxes are collected to go toward the debt. The only way the debt can be eliminated is for the government to cancel the debt itself and take back issuing money itself. This is an idea for the youth to consider and perhaps solve.

The best thing you can do is reduce your interest payments as best as you can within your day-to-day living. Don't borrow money unnecessarily. Don't use credit just for convenience.

Truth #3: Cut Out the Middle Man for the Best Value

Know that every step along the food chain has price inflation due to bank interest charges. You can develop a strategy to help yourself always pay the best price for your products.

Always cut out the middle man when you can and you will save the cost of the bank interest and the profit made by that person.

For example, we go back to our Ruby's pants illustration. If Ruby decided to import her own cotton cloth from the manufacturer instead of buying it from the importer, her price may be $10 more but she will save $30 on the cost added to the pants. This may make sense for Ruby as now her pants can sell for $170 and be competitive with other pants makers.

You can cut out the middle man in many areas of your life as well. Let's take a few examples.

Buying Food: When you buy food from the big store, it has already gone through several parts of the supply chain and the price has been set to include those costs. If you buy direct from the farmer at the local farmer's market you can save some money. Another way to save money is to purchase in bulk. When you buy a bulk quantity, you save the higher costs with the smaller packages. Plus you can cut out the middle man when you buy from the bulk supplier. If you don't have money to buy in bulk, then get a couple friends together to chip in and split the item when you get it.

Clothing: This is another area where you can spend or save a lot of money. Don't be fooled into thinking you need to buy the latest brands every year. If you buy good quality clothes that can serve multiple purposes, then you will be better off. Consider something like a good, dark colour suit. It can be used in an office environment, a funeral, or a wedding. So forget the bright yellow suit that is only good for the New Year's Eve party. Also, never buy clothes at the beginning of the season. You should buy your clothes at the end of the season when the stores have their end-of-season sales. I buy a winter jacket just before start of spring and put it away for next winter. Finally, go to the discount outlet or duty-free shopping centers. There is a great mall I go to across the border in the U.S. where I get brand-name clothes at low prices.

Housing: When buying a house, consider buying from the owner. There are sites that list the properties as for sale by owner. The real estate agent takes a big chunk out of the house price. Owners who sell themselves, are able to pass on some savings to you, the buyer. Also, buying a house "on-plan" is much cheaper than buying a house already built. A house "on-plan" means it has not been built yet but the builder is planning on building it as part of a development. If you buy early, you can find that your house value has increased 20K, 40K or more by the time the house is actually built. Make sure you select a reputable builder when buying on plan.

Truth #4: Generosity Leads to Financial Prosperity

There is a spiritual element of prosperity that no one talks about these days openly. Basically, you hear about rappers saying they sold their soul to the devil in order to make it as a success. But that is a negative aspect of success from a spiritual outlook.

There is in fact, a godly outlook on success. The rule is simple in that to obtain a spiritual push for success, a person only needs to feed the poor and the needy, to help the downtrodden and oppressed. No soul-selling is required for this spiritual success. All that is required is the exercise of love and compassion to those who are unable to repay you for that love and compassion.

You may say that you are small and starting out, so how can you be generous? Doing so will probably mean you have to sacrifice a bit but that will mean a BIGGER unlocking of the spiritual blessing meant to come your way.

As Jesus sits in the temple, he sees two people giving money in the offering box. He points the situation out to his disciples who observe what is happening. A wealthy person comes to the offering box and drops in a wad of cash. "Ohhh, now that is a prospect for membership," the disciples are probably thinking. Then they see a poor lady come by and flip in a couple of quarters. And you suspect they think that the lady is such a cheapskate. Then Jesus corrects their vision and interpretation of the situation. He tells them that truly that lady has given more than the rich man. The disciples are momentarily stunned. How can he say that? They saw for themselves the wad of cash and the two quarters. But Jesus clarifies any doubt in their minds. He says that the rich man gave out of his abundance, which was only a tiny bit but the poor lady had nothing and gave every penny she owned. Thus she gave more than the wealthy man.

And what is implied here is that her reward is indeed the greater reward because she has given more and made the greater sacrifice.

This lesson is a spiritual one you can take away to help you on life's journey and your financial success. As you are able, give generously to the needy and the poor so that it will open more spiritual blessings on your work.

~ ~ ~ ~ ~ ~ ~ ~

We have covered some money principles that can help any youth be money smart, but I can't stop there. I have one final lesson for this chapter.

As a youth, you have a tremendous advantage to you that is called TIME. Time and the value of compound interest is your best friend. By compound interest, I am not referring to usury here but to adding more to what you already have.

Working in a job will not likely result in you getting wealthy unless it's a very specific niche job that allows you to call for a lot of money. For 95% of the population, the job will be an average type of job. So how can an average person expect to get rich as they grow older? Keep adding to your wealth every year and let it grow.

Start a part-time business while you work full time. This part-time business should be one that enables you to make money with a minimum amount of hourly investment as you will most likely be working a full-time job. Today the internet has a lot of opportunity for you to start an online business that sells items like books, CDs, training, videos, design skills, etc. If you can do an online business, then let it work for you.

What if you cannot do an online business, should you give up? No.

Today there are many brick and mortar businesses that have a distributor type model where you become like an independent sales representative or distributor. You can earn an extra income that way. Be sure that you do not have to spend a lot of money up front or order items monthly and store them in your garage. That's a big warning signal to run away from them.

The business you look for should have low start-up cost, proper training and support, no inventory costs, and they are responsible for order fulfillment. All you do is get the order and get the commission cheque.

For the very brave and entrepreneurial, you can consider starting your own business. It will take a lot of time and effort, but it may bring you lots of success and the joy of being your own boss. Just don't try to do everything yourself. Outsource the parts you are not good at so that you can really put yourself into the parts that you are good at.

I have several websites that you can visit to learn more about the concepts I mentioned above plus you can also learn about a few other things that I am passionate about such as growing your own food. Visit

www.freshfood4life.com to learn about growing your own food. Or you can visit www.breakthepovertycurse.com to learn about overcoming the spiral of poverty.
.

* * * * *

The Youth Leadership Empowerment System

A Youth Action Plan

As a young person, you have to think about where you are now in your life and the kind of life you would like for yourself at age 50. To get the kind of life you want, you've got to make a plan.

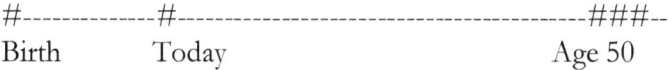
Birth　　　　Today　　　　　　　　　　　　　　　Age 50

Every person who is a success knows that success comes with the proper implementation of a plan. The power to be that kind of person lies within you. My brother had me listen to a Dale Carnegie recording called The Strangest Secret. In that recording made in the mid-1900s, Dale noted:

In a snapshot of 100 men,
At age 25, Every person said they wanted to be a success.
At age 65, One(1) Was Rich.
Four (4) Were Financially Successful.
Five (5) Were Still Working.
Fifty-Four (54) Were Broke.

Earl Nightengale goes on to say that, "Success is the progressive realization of a worthy ideal." I will say that success for my generation is getting the most out of life for the betterment of ourselves and those we care about.

~ ~ ~ ~ ~ ~ ~ ~ ~

"A humble plan, well thought out and worked diligently, will always produce rewards for the youth, or adult that is willing to achieve more in life. " - Vaughn Berkeley

"The leader has to be practical and a realist, yet must talk the language of the visionary and the idealist." - Eric Hoffer

"A youth without a plan is like a sports car without a driver. It's not going anywhere close to where it should be. " - Bryan Berkeley

~ ~ ~ ~ ~ ~ ~ ~ ~

If you are 18, 19 or 20 years old today, then you can achieve all the goals you want in life. You need to mark them down and focus on them every week. If you don't do this, then every other distraction in life will pop up to rob you of your time and energy.

The Youth Leadership Empowerment System

I'm going to break this down very simply for you.

If you want to achieve anything meaningful in your life, you must be prepared to give your life enough thought, give your dreams enough room to grow, and work diligently towards them each day of your life.

You may be totally motivated as a youth and have lots of dreams. But without a plan of action that you work daily, weekly, or monthly, you will have nothing to show for yourself year after year. And you will be like everyone else, hoping to get lucky.

This is from my brother but it is useful for anyone. I do not always follow it, but I'm following my dream in the army.

Develop an Annual Plan

In this plan, there are four areas of a youth's life. These are:
- Business
- Academics
- Personal
- Spiritual

Every year, you should try to set at least two (2) goals in each area. Each goal should be achievable within a single year. So ideally you would have 8 goals set for the year to achieve. As you get better at achieving your goals you may want to increase it to 3 per area or 4 or 5. Really, it's about your willingness to aim for the stars.

You can also have a longer goal that is a five-year goal or

ten-year goal. You need to think about how the goals for this year help you move forward toward your 5-year goal.

Let's take an example to illustrate the concept.

Johnny is 19 years old and is about to start college full time. He decides to plan his 8 goals for the year as follows:
Business:
1.	Earning $6,000 in extra income for the year.
2.	Work on dream resume.
Academic
1.	Maintain a 3.5 overall GPA.
2.	Take a university course on leadership.
Personal
1.	Exercise 3 times per week.
2.	Make 60 new friends on Facebook.
Spiritual
1.	Go to church more often.
2.	Read the scriptures more often.

Now we can look at all these goals Johnny has written and see if there are ways to help them be achieved.

For Business - 1, Johnny was clear about how much cash he wanted to make. However, without any time frame he might find himself trying a month before the end of the year to make the entire amount. A better written goal would be: Earn $1500 per quarter or $3000 per semester. Then Johnny could monitor his progress each semester.

Now let's look at Spiritual - 1, go to church more often is a great goal but there is no timeframe or way to measure the success of this. If he goes 3 times this year but went 2 last year, then he has succeeded. Again, it would be better to write the goal: Go to church on the last weekend of every month. Now Johnny has a definite time to block off in his calendar. Johnny can count the times in his calendar and know whether or not he is on track.

When working on your own goals, it is good to start with a nice broad goal but to help you monitor it and be a success, you must break it down into a goal that can be measured. Only when you are measuring your goals do you have a better chance of achieving them.

Make It a Routine to Check Your Plan Weekly

You should make it a habit to check your plan every Sunday night. Spend about an hour on it, deciding on what you will do in the coming week to get yourself closer to achieving your goals.

Let's look at Johnny. He wants to exercise three times per week. So on Sunday night, he takes out his planner and schedules in three days he will exercise. He puts in Monday, Wednesday and Friday. Oops. He noticed that Wednesday he has a group meeting during his exercise time. So he just shifts the exercise time an hour later. This is planning out his week for success.

Celebrate Your Successes

When you achieve your goal, you must celebrate your success. That does not mean doing anything to defeat your accomplished goal. For example, suppose Angela had a goal to lose 15 pounds. When Angela achieves this goal, she goes out with some friends to have a triple chocolate ice-cream delight that is sure to put on 5 pounds. Is this good? No. It will defeat her goal.

It would be the same with Johnny making $3,000 for the semester and then spending half of it on a party that was not part of his plan. His celebration of the achieved goal would have set him back.

Important Lesson: Make sure the cost of your celebration does not diminish your achievement.

Why do this?

You will see that when you begin planning your goals, you can achieve more than you would have otherwise. Perhaps you planned 12 goals per year but only ever achieved 10 of your 12. In ten years, you would have achieved 100 of your goals by your purposeful efforts. Well done. I'm sure that is more than most ordinary people would be able to say.

My brother told me he came up with this system after his first year of university. He would set 16 goals a year. He told me he would not achieve all of them. Sometimes he only achieved half and other times he achieved more. The thing is that even if he only got half the goals on this list, he often found that there were four or five other unexpected achievements that gave him great satisfaction.

And this can be the same way for you. Even if you don't achieve every goal on your plan, you will find that life brings into your path other achievements that fill you with a sense of satisfaction and joy. And these can be counted towards your "unexpected achievements."

The Youth Leadership Empowerment System

You can use the concept and guideline in this chapter to develop your own plan. I do have the actual form available for download to members of my online training program. This just makes it a bit easier for you if you don't want to design the form yourself.

* * * * *

Conclusion

I've heard my brother say that success is the sweetest revenge. He actually heard it from Tony Robbins (one of his recordings). I write this concluding chapter not as a show of revenge but to show you how everything works out for the best in the end.

This chapter is about hope for you, the reader. This book has been about four years in the making.
I started it in 2008 then stopped, then started again, then stopped and so on. Finally I was determined to have it done by 2012. And my brother was on my case about it too.

This final story happened to me in June of 2010. I had experienced a bit of a trying year up until June. I applied to get on security detail for the G20 summit in Toronto several times but was not selected.

My CO, who knew my skills and abilities and thought I was a shoe-in for the summit, asked me one time why wasn't I selected and if I had applied. I lost it and told him that I applied at least four times and that no one with coloured skin was selected. Even a new Caucasian transfer got onto the waiting list for the summit and I didn't even get on that. My CO understood my frustration and he reacted cool and understanding as he realized he hit a sore point for me. Now I am not saying that racism was involved. There may have been other factors like my age or something else. But I was still frustrated and disappointed and he knew it.

That incident blew over and I had one or two other moments that really make a young guy feel stressed. However, in June of 2010, the best experience in my military career took place. Before I tell you, let me say that I love the Canadian Armed Forces.

The army is a great place and I have had the good fortune to be among some fine soldiers and officers. I respect them highly and they know that I want to excel in the military. I even asked about what it takes to get into special ops. You could say that I'm a keener, but what can I say? I'm good at it.

So back to June of 2010. We had our final parading before we stand down for the summer. This was the time when those of us in line for promotion were given our promotions, awards of recognition were handed out and it is meant to be a good way to break for the summer.

The year before, I was fully trained and qualified to get my promotion but as circumstance would have it, I was passed over for promotion during the winter period. This time I knew that there was a strong possibility that I could get my promotion finally or perhaps I would have to wait until my training in New Brunswick. I didn't fancy the idea of having to wait again but I kind of knew the constraints on the military by now.

At the parading exercise for June, we went through the motions as per our usual routine. We had our inspection, etc. Then the senior CO came to address the troops. There were about 400 of us gathered at the exercise that evening. Our unit was about 500 strong.

Our senior CO complimented us on a job well done and went through all the military formalities. Of course, I was a bit anxious to hear the list of people being promoted as were some of my peers. He continued to talk some more about the military and then he mentioned that tonight was a very special night.

It seems that the promotions planned had never before happened in the history of our unit.

By then we were all on edge.

He was a master at how to hold us in suspense. I'm sure everyone had questions on their minds. I knew I had questions. What was this special thing that had never happened before to our unit? This something that never happened before in our unit must be something big.

Finally after a long build-up, our senior CO announced the

list of personnel to be promoted in rank that evening. He paused for what seemed like forever. Then he began to call out the list. He called out, Corporal Berkeley. Yes! Finally I would receive my promotion. Then he stopped. There were no more names on the list.

In the history of our unit, I, Bryan Berkeley, was the only person to be singly promoted. I think that God must have finally come through for me. I know my senior officers were also on my side. Out of the 400 members of my unit there, I was recognized as the only person to be promoted that evening. I was singled out as the leader among my peers, all 400 of them present. I had finally been recognized by the military I loved.

It felt good. No, it felt awesome.

There were a lot of stunned members of the unit. But my commanding officers who have known me all along were all congratulating me on a job well done and a well deserved promotion. They all knew that I was a keener. One even jokingly told me, look out CSOR, Berkeley's coming. I really like him. And I am glad to be among men of metal, courage and honour.

~ ~ ~ ~ ~ ~ ~ ~ ~

"HIGH EXPECTATIONS... are the KEY to Everything! " ~Sam Walton

"Duty makes us do things well, but love makes us do them beautifully. " - Phillips Brooks

"Patience, persistence and a good attitude will always get

you the final outcome you desire." – Bryan Berkeley

~ ~ ~ ~ ~ ~ ~ ~ ~

Leaders will eventually shine if they persist.

The fact is that I always gave the army my best. I pushed myself harder. I supported those weaker. I got discouraged a few times along the way, but I never let it shake my resolve.

In the end, I received the best reward that any person can receive at that point in their career. I, alone, was singled out for promotion that night in front of my peers.

Most of my peers were glad for me. They were expecting me to finally get my promotion and they were willing to share the joy of my moment in the spotlight. But it's not all roses. Word came back to me of one or two people being bitter about my promotion and even bad-mouthing me.

Of course, I knew who they were but I still treated them well because I said that I didn't hear it from their mouth so I'll at least give them the benefit of the doubt. But I observed them that evening and their actions reeked of jealousy. To perceive it, you need to strive to look beyond the obvious. It's too bad for them because that type of behaviour shows their lingering immaturity.

I tell you this because it is a learning experience for the budding leader you are.

When you are shining in your moment of triumph, there

may be one or two bitter people who say bad things about you.

Ignore them and don't let them spoil your well earned success.

Now I will leave you with a few instructions:
1. Never give up on your dream. Write it down and work on it a little bit each day.
2. Add me to your Facebook or Twitter. (smile) or LIKE my Facebook fan page. That way you will be close to me and perhaps I can share more insight from my own life to help you.
3. Buy copies of this book for your friends and younger family members. If you elevate those around you, then you will move up too.
4. Feel free to send me a note about your own struggles and success. I can use these in my talks to help inspire other young people. I don't care if you're 18 or 80. If you overcame, then your story can inspire someone
5. Keep re-reading and reviewing the stories in this book and the lessons learned. It is always better to learn from the mistakes and successes of others.
6. Keep moving because action produces massive results. If you keep moving towards your dream with absolute resolve, you will make it one day.

My story is still being written as is your story. It is a beautiful story. Take these lessons and have fun with it.

* * * * *

Bryan Berkeley

About The Author

Bryan is a young man on a mission in life to change the lives of young people for the better. Bryan is a youth with passion. He is a dedicated leader to which many of his military peers can attest. He is a highly skilled soldier in hand to hand combat, military weapons, explosives, and city warfare.

Bryan is also a budding actor and has already been

featured in a couple of indie movies. Though his military career keeps him busy full-time these days, he intends to take on future roles should the opportunity arise.

Bryan has been an entrepreneur for since starting high school. If there was money to be made on belt buckles, the latest baseball caps, or any teen need, he was there. He is truly a hustler as young people would say.

Bryan is also a speaker on youth issues. Bryan loves helping those around him and goes to great lengths to help his friends. His guidance has helped many students overcome difficulties in their own lives. His kind and caring personal, his diligence and attention to duty, and his noble standard, endears him to all around him.

Facebook Fanpage:
https://www.facebook.com/pages/Bryan-Berkeley-CPL/199229246821530

Twitter: bryanberkeley
Email: info@youthleadershipempowermentsystem.com

Amazon Author Page:
http://www.amazon.com/Bryan-Berkeley/e/B00C1RBFK4

Be sure to register in the
online training to learn the
Youth Leadership Empowerment System™
www.youthleadershipempowermentsystem.com

* * * * *

Youth Leadership Empowerment System Portal (www.youthleadershipempowermentsystem.com)

This site is your one-stop for access to the youth leadership empowerment system developed by Bryan Berkeley. It is a place for anyone from ages 14 to 30 to gain insights to help them develop their own leadership potential.

EternityWatch Magazine (www.eternitywatchmagazine.com)

EternityWatch Magazine is the premier magazine for those seeking a truly holistic approach to health and wellness. The magazine is founded on the belief that good health is everyone's birthright and that by proper education, people can make the right choices to maintain their good health. The magazine is focused on plant-based nutrition thus it caters to the rapidly growing vegan, and raw/living foods movement. You can get it free online just by signing up for it.

Eating4Eternity.org (www.eating4eternity.org)

Eating4Eternity is founded by Jenny Berkeley and is focused on her personal coaching approach. On the site, you will find news articles on health and wellness, Jenny's blog posts with her personal insights into what is happening in the medical field, paid courses and webinars, and some free information.

FreshFood4Life.com (www.freshfood4life.com)

Fresh food for life is part of living a healthy life. This website has information about a revolutionary garden solution for the home own with no space. You can view videos, articles and order your own garden system. You can grow 24 crops in your very own kitchen. I have one of these and so can you.

CM Berkeley Media Group
(www.cmberkeleymediagroup.com)
This is the website for anyone interested in becoming an author. It contains some great insights into the writing industry, resources for new authors, and a online course to teach you how to write your book in 90 days. The course is worth 10 times what they charge for it.

Living Food Conference
(www.livingfoodconference.com)
This is the website for anyone interested in their living food experience to the next level.

123 Contests
(www.123contests.com)
This is the website for anyone interested in running a contest to help promote a cause, promote their website, or even a new product.

* * * * *